from moa
to dinosaurs

explore & discover
ancient New Zealand

by Gillian Candler
illustrated by Ned Barraud

pb potton & burton

For my brother Andrew, who found the best fossil — GC
For Graham, always a source of inspiration — NB

Gillian Candler is an award-winning author who brings her knowledge and skills in education and publishing to her passion for the natural world. She has always been intrigued by how New Zealand must have looked to the very first people who set foot here, and wanted to find out more about what animals lived here then. She found her first fossil when she was 5 years old – an experience she'll never forget – and it opened up a whole new world of interest.

Ned Barraud is an illustrator with a keen passion for the natural world. For him, this book was a perfect opportunity to put on paper some of the most bizarre and fascinating creatures from New Zealand's past. Ned lives in Wellington with his wife and three children.

other books in the explore & discover series

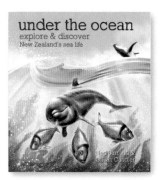

Many thanks to Alan Tennyson for his advice on the text and illustrations. The maps on pages 6–7 are based on those in George Gibbs' book, *Ghosts of Gondwana: A history of life in New Zealand*.

First published in 2016 by
Potton & Burton
98 Vickerman Street, PO Box 5128, Nelson,
New Zealand
www.pottonandburton.co.nz

Illustrations © Ned Barraud; text © Gillian Candler

ISBN PB 978 0 947503 09 3; HB 978 0 947503 10 9

Printed in China by Midas Printing International Ltd

contents

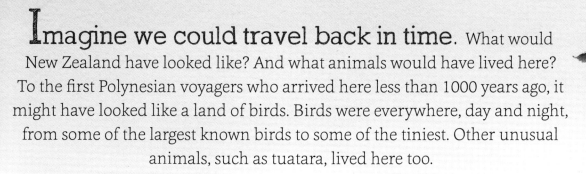

Imagine we could travel back in time. What would New Zealand have looked like? And what animals would have lived here? To the first Polynesian voyagers who arrived here less than 1000 years ago, it might have looked like a land of birds. Birds were everywhere, day and night, from some of the largest known birds to some of the tiniest. Other unusual animals, such as tuatara, lived here too.

Going further back in time over millions of years, the shape and size of the land has been through many changes. We would see crocodilians in lakes, giant penguins and shark-toothed dolphins in the seas and, many millions of years before them, dinosaurs roaming the continents of Zealandia and Gondwana.

Fossils and rocks leave clues about the changing shape of the land and the animals and plants that lived here.

Turn the page to travel back in time.

5

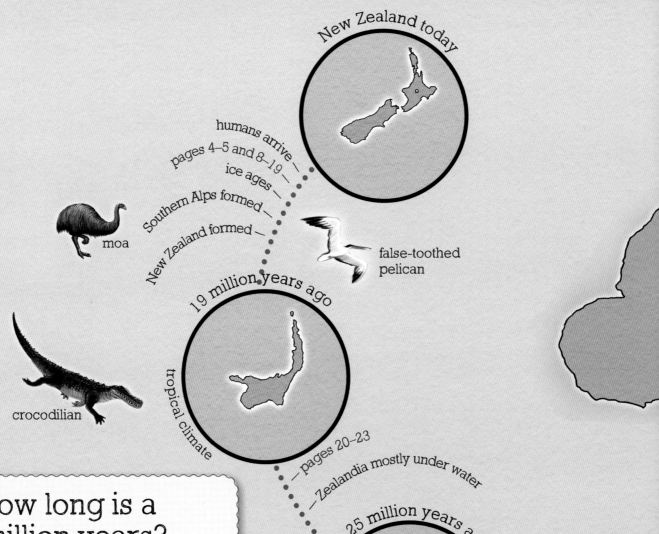

New Zealand today

humans arrive —
pages 4–5 and 8–19 —
ice ages —
Southern Alps formed —
New Zealand formed —

moa

false-toothed pelican

19 million years ago

crocodilian

tropical climate

— pages 20–23

— Zealandia mostly under water

25 million years ago

— pages 24–27

how long is a million years?

A million years is a very, very, very long time. People have lived in New Zealand for less than a thousand years. Imagine time stretching back, another thousand and another thousand years, until you have a thousand thousands stretching back in time. That is one million years. Try this: time how long it takes you to count to 100, then multiply this by 10,000. That is how long it would take you to count to one million.

shark-toothed dolphin

the changing land

New Zealand has not always been the shape it is today. Going back through time, we would see all sorts of changes – mountains rising, ice ages, tropical periods and the sea level rising and falling.

The islands that make up New Zealand today are part of the continent of Zealandia, much of which is now under the ocean. Many millions of years ago, Zealandia was part of a much, much larger continent called Gondwana. Follow the timeline to see how the shape of the land has gradually changed over time.

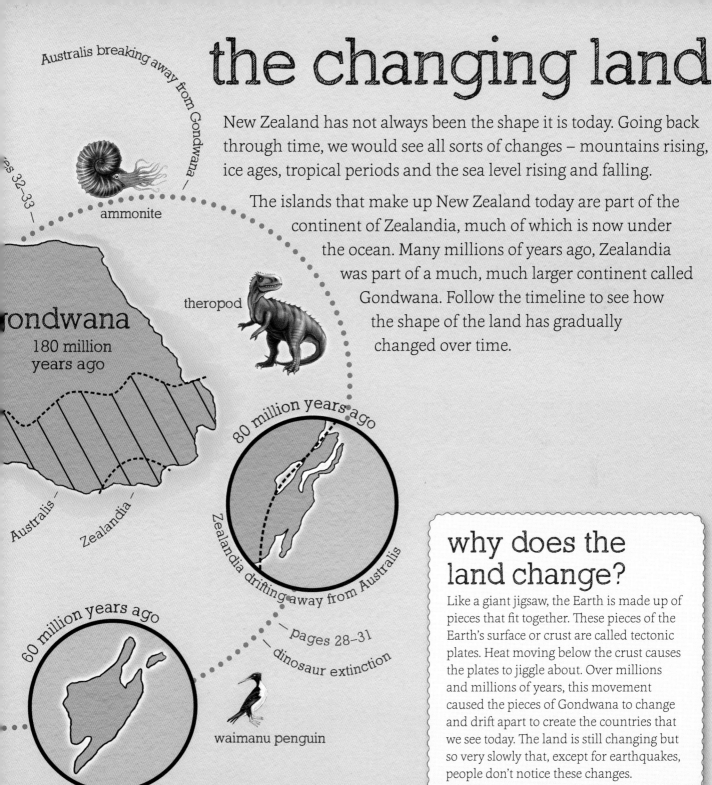

Australis breaking away from Gondwana

es 32–33

ammonite

theropod

ndwana
180 million years ago

Australis

Zealandia

80 million years ago

Zealandia drifting away from Australis

pages 28–31

dinosaur extinction

60 million years ago

waimanu penguin

why does the land change?

Like a giant jigsaw, the Earth is made up of pieces that fit together. These pieces of the Earth's surface or crust are called tectonic plates. Heat moving below the crust causes the plates to jiggle about. Over millions and millions of years, this movement caused the pieces of Gondwana to change and drift apart to create the countries that we see today. The land is still changing but so very slowly that, except for earthquakes, people don't notice these changes.

A thousand or so years ago, in ancient forests,
an orchestra of birds filled the air with warbles, chimes and haunting calls.
Huia used their curved beaks to seek out insects and forage for berries
from the trees. At the forest edge, the huge adzebill hunted frogs, lizards
and small birds. In the streams and wetlands, fish such as the kōkopu and
grayling swam and mayflies danced above the water.

8

how do we know?

Some animals such as grayling, huia, piopio and NZ quail became extinct in the last 100 years or so. People drew pictures and wrote descriptions of them, and stuffed birds were displayed in museums. Tests on fossil bones of the adzebill show they were carnivores.

At night the forest was alive with birds, bats and creatures such as giant snails. The flightless kiwi and kākāpō searched for food in the safety of darkness, away from the eyes of the giant eagle. The laughing owl looked for smaller prey, such as geckos, bats and small birds like this fairy prion, which hopes to return safely to its burrow.

how do we know?

Scientists have found fossil remains of kiwi and kākāpō, so they know that the kākāpō, which is now very rare, was once a common bird. Bones and other remains found at nest sites of the laughing owl tell us what animals this now extinct bird ate.

Icy glaciers were shrinking after an ice age 20,000 years ago came to an end. As the ice retreated, grass and scrub grew, covering the mountainous areas above the edge of the forests. Giant flightless geese grazed on the grass and some moa species lived here too. Haast's eagles, the largest known eagle, hunted the large birds in the mountains and in the forest. Tiny wrens searched for insects in the scrub. Takahē were everywhere. Along with kea and scree wētā, takahē still live in the mountains today.

Turn to pages 14–19 to learn more about moa and other extinct birds, as well as some ancient survivors. Turn to page 20 to go further back in time.

how do we know?

Tomos, or holes, in the ground above limestone caves became traps for unwary birds and other animals. Scientists have found fossils of many extinct birds in these caves as well as those of frogs, geckos and bats. Moa bones have been found with marks on them made by an eagle's talons.

13

all about moa

giant moa

The **North Island giant moa** and **South Island giant moa** were different species but would have looked similar. Female giant moa were much larger than males. While giant moa females could reach 3 metres high if their necks were stretched, moa usually held their head out in front of their body. They lived in forests as well as open areas, eating leaves, fruit and twigs.

male
1 m high to top of back

female
2 m high to top of back, up to 3 m long

moa species

- People often talk about moa as if they were all the same kind of bird, but scientists now know that there were nine different species.

- For many years scientists thought there were many more than nine species until they discovered that males and females of some species were quite different sizes.

- The **upland moa** on page 13 lived in mountains of the South Island. It had feathered legs, which would have helped to keep it warm.

- The **little bush moa** on page 9 was the most widespread of all the moa. It was common in forest on both North and South islands.

heavy-footed moa

up to 1.2 m long

The latin name for this moa means 'elephant-footed'. It was a heavy, round moa with big feet, and was only found in the South Island. A related species called **Mantell's moa** was only found in the North Island.

crested moa

The crested moa's skull had holes at the top front, which would have held a crest of feathers. Fossils and remains of this moa are rare and are only found in the South Island.

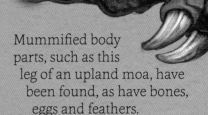

Mummified body parts, such as this leg of an upland moa, have been found, as have bones, eggs and feathers.

eastern moa

The eastern moa had a long windpipe, which meant it would have had a loud, deep call. It is thought to have lived in flocks, at least for some of the year.

up to 1 m long

stout-legged moa

female
up to 1 m long

male
up to 0.5 m long

Some stout-legged moa weighed up to 100 kilograms, others weighed as little as 9 kilograms.

moa facts

- Moa couldn't fly. Unlike other flightless birds, such as kiwi, they didn't even have wing bones.
- Moa ate plant material such as leaves, twigs and fruit.
- Moa bones were first discovered by scientists in the 1830s. Moa remains have been found in swamps, caves, sand dunes and middens (rubbish piles).
- The first people who arrived from Polynesia, founders of Māori tribes, hunted the moa for food. In just a couple of hundred years of hunting, the moa became extinct by around the 1400s.
- Since then some people claim to have seen moa in remote parts of New Zealand, and it is possible that some moa lived on into the 1800s, but some sightings were probably hoaxes.

15

other extinct birds

Haast's eagle

With males weighing up to 10 kilograms and females weighing up to 15 kilograms, Haast's eagle was the world's largest eagle. Once the moa and other large birds, such as South Island geese, were extinct, the eagles would have struggled to find enough food to eat.

claws (talons) up to 90 mm long

laughing owl

whēkau

The last sighting of a whēkau was in 1914. It was named laughing owl by Europeans for the noise that it made, but its call was more like a shriek than a happy laugh.

extinct bird facts

- Since the arrival of people, first from Polynesia and then from Europe, around 50 New Zealand bird species have become extinct.

- Extinctions were caused by people hunting birds for food and by the introduction of predators, such as rats, stoats and cats.

- Polynesians brought the kiore (rat) with them. Europeans, who began to arrive from 1769, brought the Norway and ship rats, stoats and cats with them. Mammal predators found it easy to catch and kill flightless or semi-flightless birds.

- Nearly half of the extinct species were birds that lived on the ground – rails, ducks and geese, including the huge flightless geese on page 12.

Finsch's duck

Once a very common duck, Finsch's ducks were relatives of the still-living Australian wood duck. Fossils show that over time the Finsch's duck became flightless – its wings got shorter and shorter. It lived mostly on land eating leaves, grass and other vegetation.

female

huia

male

Male and female huia had quite different shaped beaks. They lived in North Island forests eating insects, berries and leaves. They have been extinct since at least the 1920s. They were named after their call.

bush wren
mātuhi

Extinct since 1972, bush wrens were tiny birds. Also extinct are the long-billed wren, stout-legged wren and Lyall's wren. Their closest living relatives are the endangered rock wren and the rifleman.

piopio

Some people said that the piopio was one of the best singers in the New Zealand bush. It has been extinct since around 1900. Europeans called it the New Zealand thrush because it looked a bit like the thrushes in Europe.

New Zealand quail
koreke

When Europeans first arrived there appeared to be lots of koreke, but their numbers dropped quickly and they were extinct by 1875. Apart from being hunted, koreke would have been eaten by cats and rats.

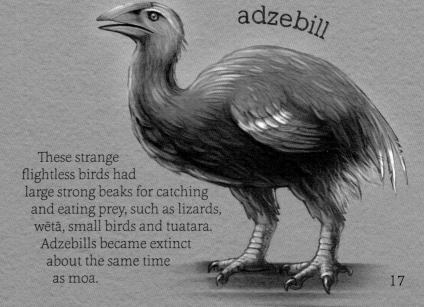

adzebill

These strange flightless birds had large strong beaks for catching and eating prey, such as lizards, wētā, small birds and tuatara. Adzebills became extinct about the same time as moa.

17

survivors from the past

giant wētā *wētā punga*

The wētā punga is one of the world's largest insects, with a body up to 10 centimetres long. The giant wētā took on a role similar to mice in a land without mammals.

kiwi

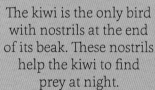

The kiwi is the only bird with nostrils at the end of its beak. These nostrils help the kiwi to find prey at night.

tuatara

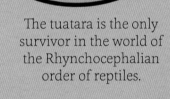

The tuatara is the only survivor in the world of the Rhynchocephalian order of reptiles.

kōkako

Along with the saddleback or tīeke, kōkako are the only survivors of an endemic wattle bird family.

native frog *pepeketua*

New Zealand's native frogs are nocturnal and can live away from water. They are the only survivors in the world of the frog family Leiopelmatidae.

18

island wildlife facts

- Isolated islands like those of New Zealand, Galapagos or Madagascar each have animals that are seen nowhere else in the world. On islands, some species become giants compared to similar species elsewhere.

- Some species, such as the tuatara, survive on isolated islands while their relatives around the world became extinct.

- Some species developed unique survival strategies not seen anywhere else in the world, such as the kiwi with its special beak or the bat that uses its wings to walk on the ground.

- In New Zealand, the only land mammals were bats. There were no other mammal predators, so many birds became flightless because they didn't need to fly to escape. When rats and other predators arrived, they had a devastating effect on the island wildlife who couldn't fly away.

batfly

short-tailed bat pekapeka

The short-tailed bat can fold its wings to use them like legs. The tiny batfly lives only with these bats – it eats bat poo and hitches a ride on the bat's fur.

scree wētā

Scree wētā live in the mountains. They freeze in the cold weather but still survive once they've thawed out.

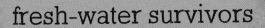
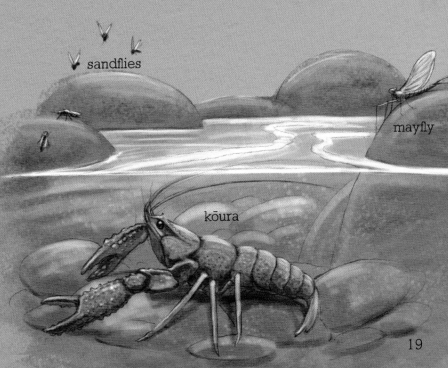

sandflies

mayfly

kōura

fresh-water survivors

Animals such as freshwater crayfish (kōura), sandflies and mayflies all depend on freshwater and can't live in sea water. Their ancestors date back to Gondwana times.

19

Around **19 million years ago**, the land that would become New Zealand had a tropical climate. There were many wetland areas and large lakes. In the warmth, gum trees and palm trees flourished. Some of the animals that lived then would be recognisable to us as ancestors of moa, kiwi and tuatara but other animals would become extinct, leaving only a few traces of their existence.

Turn the page to learn more about the animals that lived during this time, or turn to page 24 to go further back in time.

how do we know?

Scientists have found lots of fossils in what was Lake Manuherikia in Central Otago. These remains have helped them work out what animals and plants lived here in the past.

animals of lake manuherikia

Around 19 million years ago, this lake existed in Central Otago.

Fossils of **geckos** show that they were ancestors of the geckos that live in New Zealand today.

bats roosted in trees during the daytime. Several different kinds of bats have been identified from fossils. One was related to the short-tailed bat.

PAGE 19

These **turtles** lived on land and were most likely related to other large land turtles from Australia that are also now extinct.

Many different **ducks** and **wading birds** lived on or around the lake.

Fossils of the **freshwater crocodilian** suggest they may have grown to at least 3 metres in length.

Was this **parrot** an ancestor of kākā and kea? Parrot fossils were found along with those of honey-eater birds.

PAGE 35

Ancestors of the **moa** lived here. Among the bone fossils, egg shells were also found.

PAGE 14

The seas of Zealandia have always been home to unusual creatures. Around 25 million years ago, giant penguins and the ancestors of whales, dolphins and sharks swam in the ocean. At this time much of the continent of Zealandia was under water. What was left of the land would have created many islands on which land animals, such as tuatara, could survive.

how do we know?

Scientists have found fossils of ancient penguins, whales, dolphins and sharks. Fossils of shells and other marine creatures show which parts of the land were once submerged and roughly when that was.

Turn the page to learn more about ancient sea creatures, or turn to page 28 to go further back in time.

ancient sea creatures

kairuku penguin

This giant penguin lived 26–27 million years ago. It was bigger than an emperor penguin – the world's largest living penguin.

false-toothed pelican

The bill of the false-toothed pelican had serrated edges that looked like teeth. Fossils show that they lived between 3 and 53 million years ago.

wingspan up to 6 m

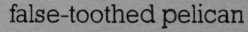

waimanu penguin

The oldest known penguin-like fossils are 60–62 million years old. The waimanu penguin was about the same size as today's hoiho or yellow-eyed penguin.

ancient sea creature facts

- Much of the land that forms New Zealand was once under water, so fossils of sea creatures can now be found on land.
- Fossils found include squid, shellfish and other small creatures, some of which lived hundreds of millions of years ago.
- Animals on these pages all lived some time between 3 and 62 million years ago, but not necessarily at the same time as each other.
- Many different species of penguin lived here, including some giant penguins, but for some species only one or two fossil bones have been found.

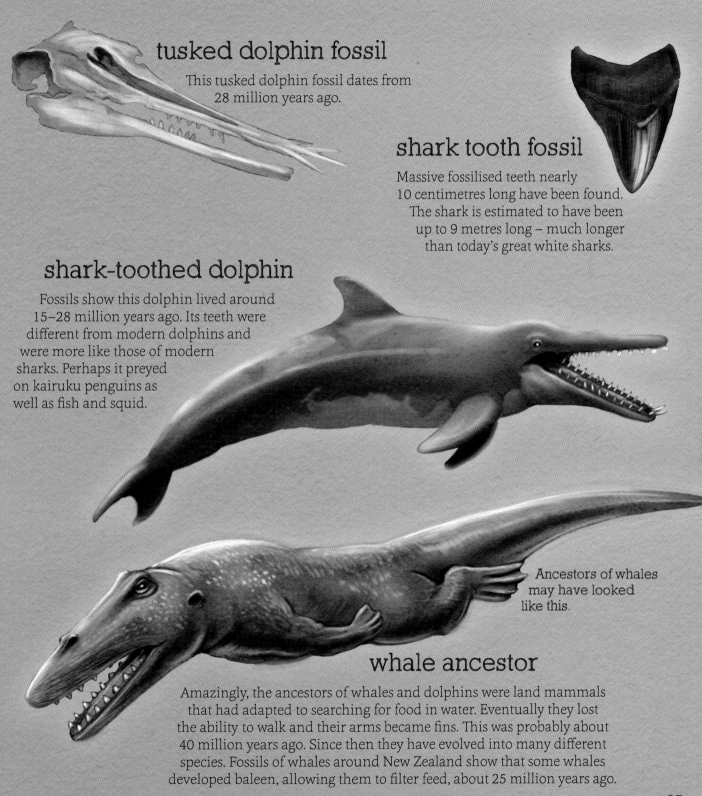

tusked dolphin fossil

This tusked dolphin fossil dates from 28 million years ago.

shark tooth fossil

Massive fossilised teeth nearly 10 centimetres long have been found. The shark is estimated to have been up to 9 metres long – much longer than today's great white sharks.

shark-toothed dolphin

Fossils show this dolphin lived around 15–28 million years ago. Its teeth were different from modern dolphins and were more like those of modern sharks. Perhaps it preyed on kairuku penguins as well as fish and squid.

Ancestors of whales may have looked like this.

whale ancestor

Amazingly, the ancestors of whales and dolphins were land mammals that had adapted to searching for food in water. Eventually they lost the ability to walk and their arms became fins. This was probably about 40 million years ago. Since then they have evolved into many different species. Fossils of whales around New Zealand show that some whales developed baleen, allowing them to filter feed, about 25 million years ago.

Around **80 million years ago**, Zealandia was joined to Australis (Australia, Antarctica and South America). Slowly, the Tasman Sea began forming and Zealandia began to drift away, taking with it plants and animals that already lived here.

The animals would have included dinosaurs, such as sauropods and theropods, that roamed the land. Pterosaurs flew in the sky and mosasaurs and plesiosaurs swam in the ocean. Along with all the large animals in the world, these animals became extinct around 65 million years ago. Only small animals such as the tuatara's ancestors, tiny mammals and the small dinosaurs that would become birds, survived.

Turn the page to learn more about animals from 80 million years ago, or turn to page 32 to go further back in time.

how do we know?

Fossils of marine and flying reptiles have been found. Fragments of dinosaur fossils give scientists clues about what dinosaurs might have lived here.

dinosaurs & more

Around 80 million years ago

tree ferns and the ancestors of kauri trees would have been in the forests of Zealandia and Australis.

PAGE 18

Although there are no fossils from this period, it is almost certain that ancestors of the **tuatara** would have lived here during this time.

PAGE 33

The first fossilised bone from a dinosaur found in New Zealand was probably from a **theropod** Theropods were carnivores.

The **plesiosaur** was a marine reptile, not a dinosaur. It ate fish and squid.

This **turtle** would make a good meal for the mosasaur.

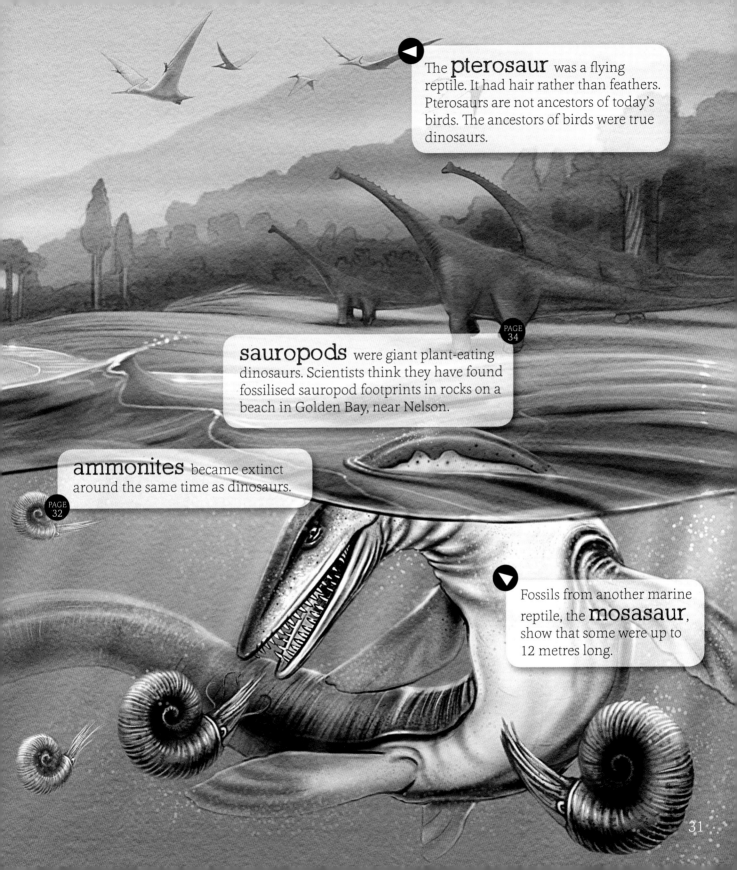

The **pterosaur** was a flying reptile. It had hair rather than feathers. Pterosaurs are not ancestors of today's birds. The ancestors of birds were true dinosaurs.

sauropods were giant plant-eating dinosaurs. Scientists think they have found fossilised sauropod footprints in rocks on a beach in Golden Bay, near Nelson.

PAGE 34

ammonites became extinct around the same time as dinosaurs.

PAGE 32

Fossils from another marine reptile, the **mosasaur**, show that some were up to 12 metres long.

31

life on gondwana

180 million years ago, Zealandia was part of the great Gondwana continent. Dinosaurs such as sauropods lived on Gondwana, as did the ancestors of animals such as tuatara, moa, frogs and peripatus. Many of the fossils found in New Zealand today date from Gondwana times, including many sea creatures as well as fossil plants. Fossils show us some of the animals that lived in Gondwana over many millions of years.
For more information about what a fossil is, turn to page 34.

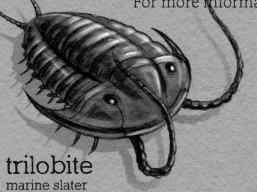

trilobite
marine slater

Trilobites are the oldest fossils found in New Zealand. The first of these fossils were found by a 14-year-old boy in a rock that is about 505 million years old.

ammonite

Rather like a squid in a shell, ammonites lived in the ocean. The largest ammonite found in New Zealand measures 1.5 metres across and is from 140 million years ago. You can see it on display at Te Papa.

fossilised forest

Fossils of fallen trees and tree stumps have been found on a beach at Curio Bay in the Catlins. About 180 million years ago, these trees were on the coast of Gondwana.

how did they get here?

Some of the unusual animals found in New Zealand would have been here ever since Zealandia split from Gondwana. However, many animals and plants arrived here after the land separated. How is this possible? Some birds, bats and insects may have flown here from Australia, or been blown here in storms. Birds may have brought seeds or insects with them. Fallen trees and vegetation could also float here from Australia on currents after storms. Once in New Zealand, if they survived, the plants and animals would change and adapt with time to their new habitat.

theropod

This theropod toe bone was found by Joan Wiffen, who discovered New Zealand's first dinosaur fossils. Most dinosaur fossils found in New Zealand are around 75 million years old.

fossilised fern

Ferns were a common plant across Gondwana.

fossilised shells

Shellfish such as brachiopods can be found in rock that was once under water. These fossils are about 400 million years old, but live brachiopods can also be found in the sea today.

rhynchocephalian fossil

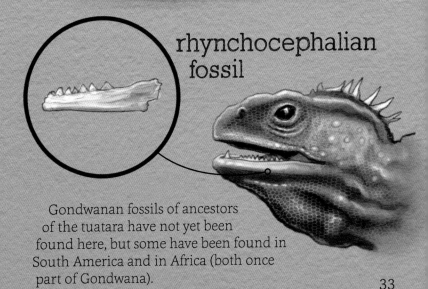

Gondwanan fossils of ancestors of the tuatara have not yet been found here, but some have been found in South America and in Africa (both once part of Gondwana).

uncovering the secrets of the past

what are fossils?

Dead plants or animals that have been quickly covered by sand, mud or volcanic ash will leave behind traces of bones or a leaf shape in any rock that forms when the sand, mud or ash hardens. Fossils can remain buried for years until earthquakes or erosion change the land and the fossils are exposed. Not every dead animal or plant leaves a fossil. There are also many fossils that will never be found.

fossil facts

- Fossils can be found in limestone caves because the limestone helps to preserve them.
- Fossils can include pollen from plants, leaves, tiny creatures, animal poo and teeth.
- Fossilised footprints are formed when an animal walks over soft sand or mud, which then hardens and is covered over by other material.
- Fossils of single bones are often found, for example, a jaw or a thigh bone. Scientists need to know a lot about animal skeletons to work out which type of animal the bone comes from.

Perhaps sauropods left these footprints in the sand.

how do scientists study the past?

Scientists who study the past are like detectives. They use clues they find in the rocks to piece together what lived in the past and when. Different types of rocks – limestone, volcanic rock, mudstone – tell a story about where the rocks came from. Fossils in the rock, even tiny ones such as pollen and little sea creatures, can give clues about how old the rocks are.

Scientists can also use morphology – the study of animal structure – and DNA to trace the ancestors of an animal and family trees of species. Scientists used morphology to determine that birds are descended from dinosaurs.

kiwi, moa and family

tinamous

kiwi

elephant bird

moa

Although kiwi and moa have the same distant ancestor, DNA shows that kiwi are more closely related to Madagascar's extinct elephant bird and moa to the South American tinamous. Moa may well have been here since Gondwanan time, however it is thought that the kiwi ancestor flew to New Zealand around 50 million years ago. Once here, the kiwi was able to survive without needing to fly, so became flightless and nocturnal.

DNA shows that kākāpō, kea and kākā are all related. Around 60–80 million years ago the kākāpō and kākā evolved from the same ancestor. And then around 3 million years ago, kea evolved by adapting to the new mountain environments. Kākāriki are much more recent arrivals in New Zealand, flying here from New Caledonia about half a million years ago.

parrot ancestors

kākāpō

kākā

kea

kākāriki

glossary

ancestor An animal's parents, grandparents, great grandparents and so on

baleen Threads that hang in curtains around the edge of a whale's jaw that enable it to filter feed

carnivore An animal that eats other animals

continent A large landmass, the size of Australia or larger

DNA Material contained in every cell of an animal or plant. It contains genes, which are information about that particular animal or plant and can be used to work out who its ancestors were.

evolved The process whereby a species adapts to its environment over many generations by changing shape or function

extinct No longer any living members of a particular species

filter Remove tiny pieces of food out of the ocean

hoax A trick to make someone believe something that isn't true

ice age A period in time lasting many years in which temperatures were much colder than those today

mammal A warm-blooded animal whose females feed their babies milk from their bodies

mummified Something, such as a body part, that has been preserved by drying out instead of decaying

nocturnal An animal that is active at nighttime

predator An animal that hunts and eats other animals

submerged Completely under water

index

find out more

Visit your local museum or fossil site, check out books from your local library or go to these websites:

gns.cri.nz/Home/Learning/Science-Topics/Fossils for information about New Zealand fossils

nzbirdsonline.org.nz for information about New Zealand birds, including extinct birds

sciencelearn.org.nz for information about New Zealand scientists and science for schools

teara.govt.nz Te Ara – the encyclopaedia of New Zealand

tepapa.govt.nz Museum of New Zealand Te Papa Tongarewa

Information for parents and teachers about this book, including more websites and activities:
www.pottonandburton.co.nz/from-moa-to-dinosaurs